THE LITTLE RED BOOK OF

KITCHEN WISDOM

THE LITTLE RED BOOK OF

KITCHEN WISDOM

Edited by Nicole Frail &
Matthew Magda

Illustrations by Kerri Frail

Skyhorse Publishing

Skyhorse Publishing books may be purchased in bulk at special discounts for sales promotion, corporate gifts, fund-raising, or educational purposes. Special editions can also be created to specifications. For details, contact the Special Sales Department, Skyhorse Publishing, 307 West 36th Street, 11th Floor, New York, NY 10018 or info@skyhorsepublishing.com.

Skyhorse® and Skyhorse Publishing® are registered trademarks of Skyhorse Publishing, Inc.®, a Delaware corporation.

www.skyhorsepublishing.com

10 9 8 7 6 5 4 3 2 1

Library of Congress Cataloging-in-Publication Data is available on file.

ISBN: 978-1-62636-082-2

Printed in China

To our parents,

Bernadette and Jeff

and

Walter and Marlene,

who instilled in us hearty appetites

for food, love, and life.

CONTENTS

Introduction

Food—both the eating and the preparation of—is often compared to art. It can be beautiful, it can be inspirational, it can be educational. It can take you outside your comfort zone, introduce you to new cultures, and show you that you have the courage to try something new. Examining a stunningly presented plate can make you excited to eat and inhaling just the right flavor can bring you back to simpler days and the happiest of times.

We don't have to tell you that food is necessary for basic human survival. What some people don't realize, however, is how much food influences us socially and emotionally—how much power it has over our relationships.

In her book *Things Cooks Love*, Marie Simmons wrote, "No matter how grand or humble, the kitchen is where everyone gathers, and where countless memories are made." In the years we've spent together, we've found this statement to be unquestionably true.

We've cooked together in various types of kitchens. Regardless of whether the stove heated unevenly or the counter wasn't big enough for an average-sized cutting board, we've managed to produce a number of dishes we've proudly shared with each other and our families. Sure, we encountered soupy banana

cream pies and inedible "Greek" meatballs along the way, but some of our happiest memories were made while sautéing onions and garlic, accidentally setting fire to wooden cooking utensils, and dancing to our favorite songs while washing and drying mountains of dirty pots and pans.

The time spent in the kitchen with those you love—whether you're helping plan, prep, make, bake, or clean—should be cherished. Working together to produce a (hopefully) delicious meal helps strengthen the bond between the two (or more) of you, even if you're simply working side-by-side without ever speaking a word.

Eating together is another story, but one that can have just as strong an effect on relationships of every kind. We've eaten at some of the best restaurants in the country, and we've enjoyed those experiences immensely, but we've noticed along the way that regardless of the amount of money we spend on the food we eat from one week to another, the only thing that really matters is the company you keep during the meal.

So cook together, bake together, eat together, and drink together. Go out and order a twenty-course tasting menu, pack a few sandwiches to devour in the park, settle into a booth at your favorite pizza place, or bring a bottle of wine home and enjoy it with takeout on the couch. Don't worry so much about the type of food you're consuming, the numbers after the dollar sign on the bill, or checking into the restaurant on social media sites so everyone knows where you are. Instead, focus on the person or people you're with and simply enjoy what you're eating.

—NICOLE FRAIL & MATTHEW MAGDA
New York City, November 2013

1

FOR THE LOVE OF FOOD

We love to eat. We love to drink. And we love to tell people about it. We take photographs of plates that impress us, we recommend restaurants, food trucks, and stands others *have* to try (whether we're asked to do so or not), and some of us even plan vacations based on when we can get reservations at restaurants on our proverbial bucket lists. In this section, we bring you thoughts on why we go out of our way to consume the best of the best, why professionals put their hearts and souls into producing plates to be proud of, and how our favorite foods and drinks make us feel when we see them, smell them, and are finally allowed to taste them.

———

No man in the world has more courage than the man who can stop after eating one peanut.
—CHANNING POLLOCK, *American playwright*

• • •

Food—because of the fact that you ingest it and not just look at it—has a unique impression on people. Because it goes across your tongue, because taste and smell are the most evocative of our senses, we react in strongly animal ways [. . .] Taste and smell are something we have to reckon with carefully.
—RICK BAYLESS, for *Culinary Artistry*

• • •

The discovery of a new dish does more for the happiness of mankind than the discovery of a star.
—JEAN ANTHELME BRILLAT-SAVARIN, *The Physiology of Taste*

• • •

Cooking is like love. It should be entered into with abandon or not at all.
—HARRIET VAN HORNE, American journalist

• • •

There is no love sincerer than the love of food.
—GEORGE BERNARD SHAW, *Man and Superman*

• • •

No sooner had the warm liquid, and the [Madeleine] crumbs with it, touched my palate than a shudder ran through my whole body, and I stopped, intent upon the extraordinary changes that were taking place. An exquisite pleasure had invaded my senses. [. . .] This all-powerful joy.
—MARCEL PROUST, *In Search of Lost Time*

• • •

A good recipe is written by someone who likes to eat and who knows how to cook—and that love and knowledge shine through.
—SUSAN DERECSKEY, *The Hungarian Cookbook*

• • •

Love is the jelly to sunshine's peanut butter. And if I tell you that I'm in sandwich with you, I'm not just saying it to get in your Ziploc bag.
—JAROD KINTZ, *Love Quotes for the Ages. Specifically Ages 18–81.*

• • •

You can develop taste, but passion is certainly a genetic thing, like a good ear for music.
—JUDITH JONES to DIANE JACOB, *Will Write for Food*

• • •

Wherefore do ye spend money for that which is not bread? [. . .]
Eat that which is good, and let your soul delight itself in fatness.
—ISAIAH 55:2

• • •

Non-cooks think it's silly to invest two hours' work in two minutes' enjoyment, but if cooking is evanescent, well, so is the ballet.
—JULIA CHILD

• • •

Food for thought is no substitute for the real thing.
—WALT KELLY, American animator and cartoonist

• • •

We've come to believe that a great dining experience is more on part with great music than with any other art. Great meals, like great music, have a rhythm and harmony all their own.
—KAREN PAGE, in the preface of *Culinary Artistry*

• • •

When you acknowledge, as you must, that there is no such thing as perfect food, only the idea of it, then the real purpose of striving toward perfection becomes clear: to make people happy. That's what cooking is all about.
—THOMAS KELLER, *The French Laundry Cookbook*

• • •

The Ultimate Picky Eater

"I am, let's face it, not the best eater. I don't like foods touching, I insist that meat, fish, and even fowl be perilously rare, and I know how to say 'sauce on the side' in five languages. When I was a kid, my diet consisted of American cheese slices that I would not eat unless they had been cut into pretty shapes. On my birthday, I was allowed to skip dinner."
—PATRICIA MARX, "A Not-So-Simple Plan,"
The New York Times

• • •

Eggs Benedict is genius. It's eggs covered in eggs. I mean, come on, that person should be the president.
—WYLIE DUFRESNE, wd~50

• • •

There is no spectacle on Earth more appealing than that of a beautiful woman in the act of cooking dinner for someone she loves.
—TOM WOLFE

• • •

Food depends on life, sustains and takes life, enhances, documents, influences, and affirms life. But the most fascinating aspect of food is its connection to all aspects of living.
—CAROL W. MAYBACH, *Creating Chefs*

• • •

The human craving for flavor has been a largely unacknowledged and unexamined force in history. Royal empires have been built, unexplored lands have been traversed, great religions and philosophies have been forever changed by the spice trade. In 1942, Columbus set sail to find seasoning. Today, the influence of flavor in the world marketplace is no less decisive. The rise and fall of corporate enemies [. . .] is frequently determined by how their products taste.
—ERIC SCHLOSSER, *Fast Food Nation*

• • •

Writers know that if you want to portray a person succinctly, tellingly, you describe the way he eats.
—AMANDA HESSER, *Eat, Memory*

• • •

I was born with a taste in my mouth, in much the same way that a songwriter is born with a tune in his head.
—PETER KAMINSKY, *Culinary Intelligence*

• • •

I may never be happy, but tonight I am content. Nothing more than an empty house, the warm hazy weariness from a day spent setting strawberry runners in the sun, a glass of cool sweet milk, and a shallow dish of blueberries bathed in cream.
—SYLVIA PLATH, *The Unabridged Journals of Sylvia Plath*

• • •

"I want you to try to remember what brought you comfort when you were younger."
Bowls of cereal after school, coated in a pool of orange-blossom honey. Dragging my finger along the edge of a plate of mashed potatoes. I knew I should have thought "tea" or "bath," but I didn't.
"Grilled cheese?" I said hesitantly.
"Okay, good. What else?"
—STEPHANIE KLEIN, *Straight Up and Dirty: A Memoir*

• • •

She stuck her head out and took a deep breath. If she could eat the cold air, she would. She thought cold snaps were like cookies, like gingersnaps. In her mind they were made with white chocolate chunks and had a cool, brittle vanilla frosting. They melted like snow in her mouth, turning creamy and warm.
—SARAH ADDISON ALLEN, *The Sugar Queen*

• • •

All you need is love. But a little chocolate now and then doesn't hurt.
—CHARLES M. SCHULZ

• • •

One cannot think well, love well, sleep well, if one has not dined well.
—VIRGINIA WOOLF, *A Room of One's Own*

• • •

Humor keeps us alive. Humor and food. Don't forget food.
You can go a week without laughing.
—JOSS WHEDON, American screenwriter and producer

• • •

I am not a glutton—I am an explorer of food.
—ERMA BOMBECK, American humorist

• • •

I love the ritual of eating. How the way you hold your knife
and fork (or chopsticks or fingers), and what you choose
to put between them, determines so much about who
you are, where you are from, how you came to be eating
this very meal.
—GAIL SIMMONS, *Talking with My Mouth Full*

• • •

Good food is the foundation of genuine happiness.
—AUGUSTUS ESCOFFIER

• • •

A good night sleep, or a ten minute bawl, or a pint of
chocolate ice cream, or all three together, is good medicine.
—RAY BRADBURY, *Dandelion Wine*

• • •

Am I tough? Am I strong? Am I hard-core? Absolutely.
Did I whimper with pathetic delight when I sank my teeth
into my hot fried-chicken sandwich? You betcha.
—JAMES PATTERSON, *The Angel Experiment*

• • •

I moan with pleasure.
"Did you just have a foodgasm?" he asks, wiping ricotta
from his lips.
"Where have you been all my life?" I ask the beautiful panini.
—STEPHANIE PERKINS, *Anna and the French Kiss*

• • •

Everything you see I owe to spaghetti.
—SOPHIA LOREN, Italian actress

• • •

Pull up a chair. Take a taste. Come join us.
Life is so endlessly delicious.
—RUTH REICHL, American food critic

• • •

2

MAIN INGREDIENTS

These days, it seems that grocery storefronts, celebrity chefs, and cookbook authors all preach about the significance of superior products. Many people see this movement as a simple ploy to have us spend more money on organic "this" and GMO-free "that," but the truth is this: the level of your ingredients *is* almost as important as your skill as a cook. Producers, artisans, and farmers spend their lives working to provide you with the best products they can, so go ahead and spend a few extra dollars if you can afford to. Lift your food to the next level and treat yourself and your family with superior extra virgin olive oil or a few pounds of Wagyu beef. This section includes quotes about favorite or key ingredients, foods cooks can't seem to get enough of, and flavor combinations that will make your mouth water.

Spaghetti is love.
—MARIO BATALI

Ingredient lists should not be as long as nineteenth-century Russian novels unless you're cooking for the czar, in which case, good luck finding Favergé plates at your local Wal-Mart.
—KASEY WILSON, co-host, *The Best of Food and Wine*

• • •

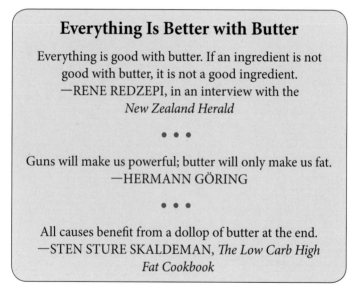

Everything Is Better with Butter

Everything is good with butter. If an ingredient is not good with butter, it is not a good ingredient.
—RENE REDZEPI, in an interview with the
New Zealand Herald

• • •

Guns will make us powerful; butter will only make us fat.
—HERMANN GÖRING

• • •

All causes benefit from a dollop of butter at the end.
—STEN STURE SKALDEMAN, *The Low Carb High Fat Cookbook*

• • •

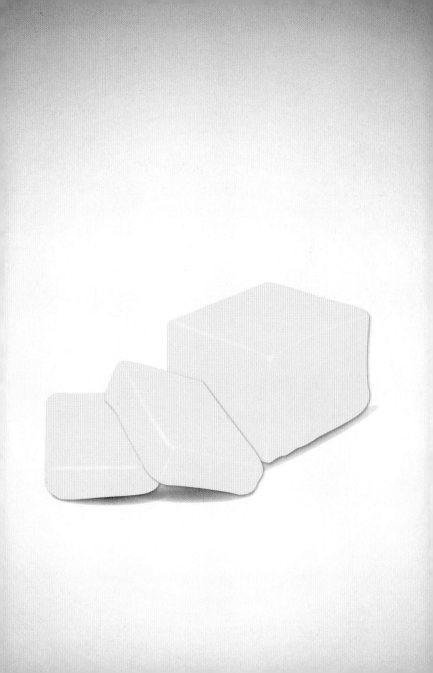

And that's the thing about grilling: The steak you make is only as good as the steak you buy. Or the pork chops. Or the chicken thighs. Or the spare ribs. Or—well, you get the point.
—ADAM RAPOPORT, on the importance of high-quality ingredients, "Editor's Letter," *Bon Appétit*

• • •

Our entire humanity would have poor health if vegetables tasted as good as bacon.
—STEN STURE SKALDEMAN, *The Low Carb High Fat Cookbook*

• • •

Foie gras and corn are made for each other: the richness of the liver pairs perfectly with the natural sweetness of the kernels.
—CHRIS COSENTINO, *Beginnings*

• • •

I could become a James Beard Award–winning food writer or a *Top Chef* Master and I will always believe the best food in the world is a simple thing called "cheese toast"—which is fancy for cheese melted on toast.
—ALYSSA SHELASKY, *Apron Anxieties*

• • •

To relax at home one night, I opened a Chinese cookbook I like, and it fell on a page on sesame seeds. So then I start thinking about tahini, maybe a black sesame tahini for the dish? There's a randomness there. I didn't open the book looking for inspiration, but now sesame is on my radar.
—WYLIE DUFRESNE to FRANCIS LAM, "The Flavorist Conversations," from Salon.com

• • •

I'm about a tablespoon of heavy cream away from having the National Dairy Council sponsor our dinner.
—JEN LANCASTER, *Such a Pretty Fat*

• • •

Eating a plain bagel with no cream cheese is like eating the inner tube of a bicycle tire, and I'd rather ride my roller skates to work.
—JAROD KINTZ, *This Book Is Not for Sale*

• • •

I don't care if you're the Great Gatsby throwing a white party in the Hamptons. There should always be potato chips! Give me some Lay's® Classics, and no matter how dry your BBQ chicken is, I'll come back.
—ANDREW KNOWLTON, "The Food List," *Bon Appétit*

• • •

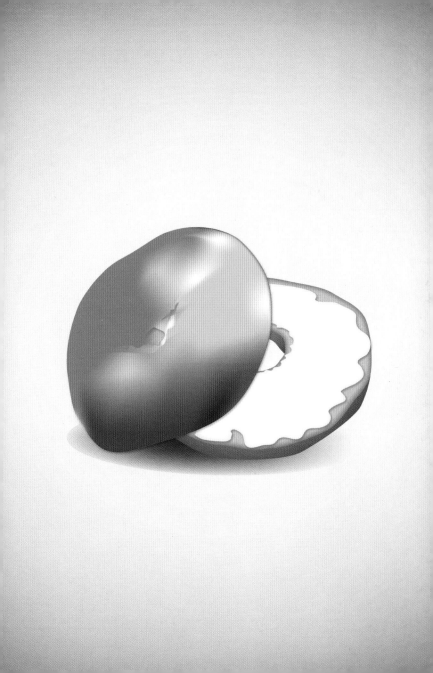

The starting point is the ingredients. What is the focus of the dish? [. . .] Whatever it is, there's something that's the reason why I'm cooking the dish. And I try not to let the dish go too far away from that reason.
—JASPER WHITE to ANDREW DORNENBURG and KAREN PAGE, authors of *Culinary Artistry*

• • •

I think the combination of chocolate and lemon is so refreshing. In England, I even tasted a yogurt flavored with chocolate and lemon. Sounds weird, tastes great!
—DIETER SCHORNER, professor at the Culinary Institute of America

• • •

The thought of spinach is pleasure. French cooks, Chinese cooks, Italian cooks, Indian cooks would all rate spinach the best of leaf vegetables.
—JANE GRIGSON, award-winning food writer

• • •

Mostly eat what has moved. And let the food hang for a while. Sixty days is about enough. If the food is still screaming after, it hasn't been hanging long enough.
—STEN STURE SKALDEMAN, *The Low Carb High Fat Cookbook*

• • •

Remember this: meat is the master. Sauce, seasoning, and smoke are its faithful servants.
—ADAM PERRY LANG, *Charred & Scruffed*

• • •

Fava beans and I have a love-hate relationship. I love it when the first pods of spring arrive in the kitchen, but I hate that it takes hours to shell them.
—CHRIS COSENTINO, *Beginnings*

• • •

An Ode to Salt

Salt is the king of tastes.
—PETER KAMINSKY, *Culinary Intelligence*

• • •

If salt was necessary, pepper was a luxury, available only to those who could afford it. These days, though, pepper seems fated to be the perpetual follower, at least in common speech. One says without thinking, "Please pass the salt and pepper."
—RICHARD SNODGRASS, on the history of salt,
Kitchen Things

• • •

People [tell me], "You never say how much salt to use." It depends on how you feel.
—FRIEDEMAN PAUL ERHARDT, as quoted in Ronald Joseph Kule's *Chef Tell*

• • •

Salt is the most fundamental taste. Without it, meat is boring. In fact, almost everything is boring. It lifts all the other flavors, the way a rising tide lifts a boat.
—ADAM PERRY LANG, *Charred & Scruffed*

• • •

The idea is to simplify cooking instead of making it more dramatic—just get down to the core of what's important. Bring out the best qualities of the food itself. Period. A dish may only need three or four things to bring out its potential.
—GLENN HUMPHREY, *Creating Chefs*

• • •

Not everything can be ready immediately just because you want it to be. [. . .] In my world, longing is the main ingredient of pleasure. When something takes time, we get a chance to long for it, and in the end, everything tastes so much better.
—SÉBASTIEN BOUDET, *The French Baker*

• • •

I have often wondered who was the first person to realize that eating an artichoke was a good idea.
—CHRIS COSENTINO, *Beginnings*

• • •

Did you know . . .?

Christopher Columbus did not embark on his voyage to prove that the world was round, but to find a more direct route to the sources of spices because of their flavors.

And . . .

The voyagers who followed in the sixteenth and seventeenth centuries were seeking not just gold, but also control of spice trade and production.
—From GORDON M. SHEPHERD'S, *Neurogastronomy*

• • •

A freezer without lamb meat is an empty freezer.
—STEN STURE SKALDEMAN, *The Low Carb High Fat Cookbook*

• • •

I suppose there are people who can pass up free guacamole, but they're either allergic to avocado or too joyless to live.
—FRANK BRUNI, *Born Round: The Secret History of a Full-time Eater*

• • •

What is soup? It is some sort of food, diluted with enough liquid for you to be able to eat the dish with a spoon. It isn't any more complicated than that.
—STEN STURE SKALDEMAN, *The Low Carb High Fat Cookbook*

• • •

Bread is the only food I know that satisfies completely, all by itself. It comforts the body, charms the senses, gratifies the soul, and excites the mind. A little butter helps also.
—JEFFREY STEINGARTEN, *The Man Who Ate Everything*

• • •

If you look at ingredients like characters in a play, there are times that there are twenty characters on stage and times when there are just two. So what you pair an ingredient [. . .] with depends on how many characters are on the stage.
—NORMAN VAN AKEN to ANDREW DORNENBURG and KAREN PAGE, authors of *Culinary Artistry*

• • •

Tomatoes and oregano make it Italian; wine and tarragon make it French. Sour cream makes it Russian; lemon and cinnamon make it Greek. Soy sauce makes it Chinese; garlic makes it good.
—ALICE MAY BROCK, restaurateur

• • •

Only when you understand and respect the essence of an ingredient can you properly come to enhance its flavor through cooking. [. . .] But the best of all cooking is when ingredients taste like themselves. A culinary artist must respect the essence of ingredients, and take care to choose those of the highest possible quality.
—ANDREW DORNENBURG and KAREN PAGE, *Culinary Artistry*

• • •

Eating better definitely doesn't mean compromising on fantastic ingredients and delicious meals.
—JAMIE OLIVER, in a review of Peter Kaminsky's *The Art of Eating Healthy*

• • •

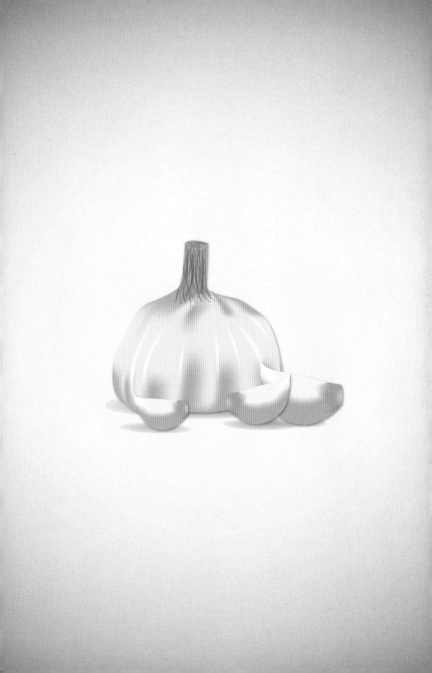

Apples and cinnamon? A love story of the most magical kind,
I might well say.
—DANIELA KLEIN, *Little Sweets and Bakes*

• • •

Foods I wouldn't touch even if I were starving on a desert
island: None, except maybe insect.
—JEFFREY STEINGARTEN, *The Man Who Ate Everything*

• • •

Asparagus is the perfect vegetable for people who want to eat
healthy. Not only does it look beautiful on the plate, but it is
delicious, inexpensive, easy to prepare, and it contains hardly
any carbohydrates. Yes, it is almost fat-free, but don't worry—
it tastes heavenly with butter, cream, and mayo.
—STEN STURE SKALDEMAN, *The Low Carb High
Fat Cookbook*

• • •

My favorite animal is steak.
—FRAN LEBOWITZ, American author

• • •

That's all a grit is, a vehicle. For whatever it is you rather
be eating.
—KATHRYN STOCKETT, *The Help*

• • •

The beet is the most intense of vegetables. The radish, admittedly, is more feverish, but the fire of the radish is a cold fire, the fire of discontent not of passion. Tomatoes are lusty enough, yet there runs through tomatoes an undercurrent of frivolity. Beets are deadly serious.
—TOM ROBBINS, *Jitterbug Perfume*

• • •

Vegetables must be eaten fresh to be good. The soil in which they were cultivated, the climate that brought them to life will sing in one's mouth . . . if they are not mangled in the cooking process. Cooking them is a delicate operation.
—HERVÉ THIS, *Kitchen Mysteries*

• • •

Grass seeds, such as barley, wheat, rye, and corn are bird food. Let the birds fatten up on bird food, then we can eat the birds. The same reasoning can be applied to cows.
—STEN STURE SKALDEMAN, *The Low Carb High Fat Cookbook*

• • •

3

METHODS TO SWEAR BY

Similar to secret ingredients, professional and home cooks alike have methods they swear by—ways of approaching recipes that pull dishes together and make the difference between delicious and mediocre. These methods may involve cooking chicken under a brick, using cast-iron pans for everything, using *only* homegrown ingredients, or following recipes as though they are carved in stone (or straying from recipes when the moment feels right!). This section will give you a little glimpse into the methods that food lovers around the world deem the best whether they're planning a meal, creating a new dish, or simply following an age-old recipe.

———

If if's and and's were pots and pans, there'd be no need for tinkers.
—GEORGE BERNARD SHAW, *Saint Joan*

• • •

Steaming is one of the gentlest ways to cook, since it is only the even, moist heat of the vapors—not simmering water—that envelops the food, allowing it to retain most of its natural juices and nutrients.
—IRMA S. ROMBAUER, MARION ROMBAUER BECKER, and ETHAN BECKER, *The All New All Purpose Joy of Cooking*

• • •

Cooking is not about convenience and it's not about shortcuts. [. . .] Take your time. Take a long time. Move slowly and deliberately and with great attention.
—THOMAS KELLER, *The French Laundry Cookbook*

• • •

I admit it gives me enormous pleasure to imagine the powers
of alchemy and sorcery that the mortar suggests—it's as if I
have the ability to transform matter and mix magic potions.
—PENELOPE CASAS, *Delicioso*

• • •

Fondue is fun to eat and an easy way to entertain. Folks love
fondue because it satisfies the primal act of sharing food with
friends. When I'm in the mood for a satisfying, informal meal,
I fire up my trusty fondue pot.
—RICK RODGERS, *Fondue*

• • •

Pizza is fun. Pizza is a synonym for *party*. Here are my instructions on how to throw a really great pizza party. Step one: Order pizza. That's it.
—JIM GAFFIGAN, *Dad Is Fat*

• • •

"Why don't you use asparagus," Thomas said. "What else do we have?"
"We have some truffle coulis," Grant said.
Thomas nodded and said, "Use asparagus and truffles."
Grant nodded. And that was how a new French Laundry dish was created.
—A conversation between THOMAS KELLER and GRANT ACHATZ, as featured in Michael Ruhlman's *The Soul of a Chef*

• • •

Recipes—to follow or not to follow? That is the question.

Trust your instincts. Use common sense when following recipes. If it calls for a pan on high heat, but the food is burning, it's probably too hot. If a piece of meat looks as if it's overcooking, it probably is, so take it out even if it hasn't been in as long as the recipe says.
—THOMAS KELLER, *The French Laundry Cookbook*

• • •

One certainly cannot learn the technical details of cookery entirely from books; but if cooks, celebrated and obscure, of the past had believed that written recipes were unnecessary, we should now be in a sad plight indeed.
—ELIZABETH DAVID, *French Provincial Cooking*

• • •

Ideally, a recipe captures the essence of the food in question, as well as the very culture of the dish and the personal interests of the recipe writer.
—ANTONIA ALLEGRA, in the foreword to *The Recipe Writer's Handbook*

• • •

PIZZA
- Dough
- Sauce
- Cheese
- Italian seasoning
- Salt & pepper

A good recipe is one that first encourages the reader to cook, and then delivers what it promises. A well-written recipe takes you by the hand and says, don't worry, it'll all be okay, this is what you're looking for.
—ELIZABETH LUARD, *The Old World Kitchen*

• • •

Recipes are important but only to a point. What's more important than recipes is how we think about food.
—MICHAEL SYMON

• • •

The process of cooking food in hot fat is only slightly less ancient than roasting a carcass on an outdoor fire. Egyptians used goose, pork, and beef fat for frying. Arabian cooks preferred the unique flavor of sheep's tail fat. Worldwide, [. . .] just about anything was better cooked in oil.
—KATY VINE, "I Believe I Can Fry," featured in *Texas Monthly*

• • •

Many devoted cooks would say that modernist cooking takes some of the joy out of our favorite pastime. [Nathan Myhrvold's] egg scrambling is antiseptic—no foaming butter, no sound when the egg hits the pan, no pride when the eggs come out great. There's just the lab-like whirring of a machine sitting on the counter.
—SOPHIE BRICKMAN, on observing the author of *Modernist Cuisine* make her eggs, "Nathan Myhrvold's Method Makes Science of Cook," as featured in *The San Francisco Chronicle*

• • •

The moral of this story is not everything that's slick is non-stick, and not everything non-stick is slick.
—ALTON BROWN, on Teflon

• • •

Strain and skim. When in doubt, strain. Not a single liquid or purée moves from one place to another at the restaurant except through some kind of strainer. And you must always be skimming—skim, skim, skim.
—THOMAS KELLER, *The French Laundry Cookbook*

• • •

Deconstruction and reconstruction of food can be very imaginative and, at times, quite nice, but I find that the whole, real products [. . .] are so complex and nuanced that I don't think I can improve on things by putting them in an atom smasher in hopes that something interesting and delicious will pop out.
—ADAM PERRY LANG, *Charred & Scruffed*

• • •

I own a few hundred pots and pans, but the one I use most frequently is a cast-iron skillet left behind by a college roommate back in the '60s. Nothing beats this skillet for cooking thick steaks or pork chops to juicy perfection.
—BRUCE AIDELIS, *The Complete Meat Cookbook*

• • •

Shopping from the gut makes me feel womanly.
—ALYSSA SHELASKY, *Apron Anxieties*

• • •

Should the preparation be placed in the freezer hot or cold?

According to Hervé This, in his book *Kitchen Mysteries*, if you're in a hurry for something to freeze or chill, you could expedite the process by making sure the liquid is warm or hot before you place it in the freezer:

"Common sense tells us that the freezer will work more efficiently if the preparation is already cold. Common sense is not always right, however. Hot water freezes more quickly than cold water."

• • •

As for what you can cook in cast iron, my answer is just about anything.
—JOANNA PRUESS, *Griswold and Wagner Cast Iron Cookbook*

• • •

I'm always thinking about food in a new way, but I'm not trying to reinvent the wheel. It's more like I'm stopping and looking again at what's been done and then presenting it my way. My food will not change the world, but I do hope you enjoy the journey.
—CHRIS COSENTINO, *Beginnings*

• • •

Grilling's one of the worst ways to cook a steak. Those grill marks you get? That's burnt. I don't care—if it's black, it's burnt. Deep, deep dark crusty brown—that's good.
—TOM COLICCHIO to SCOTT RAAB, on why roasting steak is better than grilling, *Esquire*

• • •

All sandwiches should be prepared so that every particle
is edible.
—JOANNA PRUESS, *Griswold and Wagner
Cast Iron Cookbook*

• • •

Don't overdo it. Make one great thing and a simple salad
with Grandma's dressing. Think about the colors on the plate;
make it beautiful.
—ADVICE FROM MOM, from Alyssa Shelasky's
Apron Anxieties

• • •

Roasting is one of the oldest and most spectacular forms of cooking. Originally, roasting was done on a spit in front of the fire. What we call roasting—food cooked by dry heat in the oven—was known until the end of the nineteenth century as baking.
—JAMES BEARD, *James Beard's Theory & Practice of Good Cooking*

• • •

You can pretty much make fish soup out of anything, but it always tastes better if you include fish.
—STEN STURE SKALDEMAN, *The Low Carb High Fat Cookbook*

• • •

Unless you have demolition equipment in your kitchen,
precracked is the way to go.
—PETER KAMINSKY, on working with hard-shell crabs,
Culinary Intelligence

• • •

A comedian I heard recently suggested that the best way to
get a man to cook for you is to get him to associate cooking
with danger. [. . .] If cooking involves fire or large knives
or a whole fish—preferably all three—he's there.
—SYDNEY BIDDLE BARROWS, American businesswoman

• • •

4

GROW YOUR OWN

It's important to know where the food we eat comes from. We can read labels in grocery stores, visit farmers' markets on weekends, and even join co-ops. Many chefs and restaurant owners around the world have their own plots of land where they grow the herbs and produce used in their dishes so they can offer their diners the freshest and most delicious food possible. They may also forage for the berries and truffles they use. Home cooks, whether they live in the city or country, can also grow their own seasonal ingredients. Mini farming—planting produce and herbs in small plots on roofs, balconies, or windowsills—has caught on in recent years. This section should serve to remind you to support your local farmers and eat the freshest ingredients whenever possible.

• • •

The single greatest lesson the garden teaches is that our relationship to the planet need not be zero-sum, and that as long as the sun still shines and people still can plan and plant, think and do, we can, if we bother to try, find ways to provide for ourselves without diminishing the world.
—MICHAEL POLLAN, *The Omnivore's Dilemma*

• • •

Whenever I have doubts about whether all of this effort has
been worth it, I go out into the wilds behind my backyard and
taste a fruit or flower freshly plucked from a tree or vine. [. . .]
I love the flavor of where I live.
—GARY PAUL NABHAN, *Coming Home to Eat*

• • •

I love that I can taste history with these heirloom varieties.
[. . .] Each of these varieties has a story that needs to be told.
Everything about the apple is there in the graft, in the cultivar.
It doesn't go away.
—BRIAN NICHOLASON to MICHAEL WELCH, on his
orchard's apples, for *Edible*

• • •

As long as one egg looks pretty much like another, all the chickens like chickens, and beef beef, the substitution of quantity for quality will go on unnoticed by most consumers, but it is becoming increasingly apparent to anyone with an electron microscope or a mass spectrometer that, truly, this is not the same food.
—MICHAEL POLLAN, on $2.20 pasteurized eggs versus $0.79 industrial eggs, *The Omnivore's Dilemma*

• • •

At night I dreamed of being on the cover of *Gourmet* magazine wearing a black cowboy hat and cradling a bundle of carrots. Headline: "Chefs as Farmers-Scientists: The New Frontier in Food."
—DAN BARBER, "The Great Carrot Caper," *The New York Times*

• • •

By the simple act of making a purchase of local ingredients, you are voting with your pocketbook for sustainable, often organic produce.
—PETER KAMINSKY, *Culinary Intelligence*

• • •

One of the truly odd things about the 10 billion bushels
of corn harvested each year is how little of it we eat. [. . .]
Less than a bushel per person per year.
—MICHAEL POLLAN, *The Omnivore's Dilemma*

• • •

It is a golden maxim to cultivate the garden for the nose, and
the eyes will take care of themselves.
—ROBERT LOUIS STEVENSON

• • •

It is only the farmer who faithfully plants seeds in the Spring,
who reaps a harvest in the Autumn.
—B. C. FORBES, founder of *Forbes* magazine

• • •

Food security is not in the supermarket. It's not in the government. It's not at the emergency services division. True food security is the historical normalcy of packing it in during the abundant times, building that in-house larder, and resting easy knowing that our little ones are not dependent on next week's farmers' market.
—JOEL SALATIN, author of *Folks, This Ain't Normal*

• • •

It's an empowering idea. The entire goliath of the food industry is driven and determined by the choices we make as the waiter gets impatient for our order or in the practicalities and whimsies of what we load into our shopping carts or farmers'-market bags.
—JONATHAN SAFRAN FOER, *Eating Animals*

• • •

My grandma used to plant tomato seedlings in tin cans from tomato sauce and purée and crushed tomatoes she got from the Italian restaurant by her house, but she always soaked the labels off first. "I don't want them to be anxious about the future," she said. "It's not healthy."
—BRIAN ANDREAS, author of *Traveling Light*

• • •

We must cultivate our own garden. When man was put in the garden of Eden he was put there so that he should work, which proves that man was not born to rest.
—VOLTAIRE

• • •

The best cooking is that which takes into consideration the products of the season.
—FERNAND POINT, the "Godfather of Modern Cuisine,"
Ma Gastronomie

• • •

Amid the incessant drumbeat of bad news permeating our lives these days are glimmering signs of hope, manifested at the weekly gathering at the farmers' markets, in neighborhood food gardens, in fields and orchards well tended, and on home and restaurant tables where people have once again discovered the deep satisfaction of food well grown and prepared.
—MICHAEL ABLEMAN, in the foreword to *Edible*

• • •

Hiring a farmer to manage one's land is like dating to find
a spouse.
—ILENE BEZAHLER, for *Edible*

• • •

Weather means more when you have a garden. There's nothing
like listening to a shower and thinking how it is soaking in
around your green beans.
—MARCELENE COX, American writer

• • •

5

FOR THE HOME COOK

Grandma's meatballs. Dad's stir-fry. Mom's pumpkin roll. Aunt Peg's pickles. All home cooks have at least one dish with their names on it—one their families request time and time again or one their friends ask them to bring to all get-togethers, regardless of occasion. Some home cooks follow recipes to a T, some create their own sweet and savory concoctions, and some pass their secret ingredients and methods on to their biggest fans. These men and women are most comfortable when they're up to their elbows in batter or tending to the flames at the grill. Home cooks specialize in one type of cuisine—whichever one will make those they love happy.

———

One of the joys of cooking at home is that you can switch up the menu every night. You can't always do that in a restaurant.
—MARK VETRI, *Rustic Italian Food*

• • •

Home is where you know what's in the meat stew.
—DANISH PROVERB

• • •

The more people cook, the healthier they are.
—MICHAEL POLLAN, *In Defense of Food*

• • •

Remember, you are alone in the kitchen, and no one
can see you.
—JULIA CHILD, after flipping a potato pancake onto the
work table and putting it back in the pan while filming an
episode of *The French Chef*

• • •

Pete Wells Takes on Mise en Place

The whole idea of mise en place tortures me. [. . .] In my mind, it stands as an unattainable ideal, a receding mirage, a dream of an organized and contented kitchen life that everyone is enjoying except me.

It's time for amateurs to take back the kitchen. We can start by redefining mise en place. [. . .] Simply put, nobody is going to pit olives for me [. . .] so I'll have to pit them whenever I can steal a few minutes in the midst of ambient chaos. The recipe [. . .] has to open up a little to make room for real life.
—From "Prep School," as featured in
The New York Times Magazine

• • •

Sally: Why doesn't the food taste as good when I follow one of your recipes as it does when you make it?

Todd: Why is it that a carpenter can build something far better than I could ever conceive of building that thing myself, even with the right tools and the right design? Practice makes perfect. And as Rick Pitino (the coach of the Celtics) says, "Perfect practice makes perfect."

—A conversation between SALLY SAMPSON and TODD ENGLISH, authors of *The Figs Table*

• • •

Instead of going out to dinner, buy good food. Cooking at home shows such affection. In a bad economy, it's more important to make yourself feel good.

—INA GARTEN

• • •

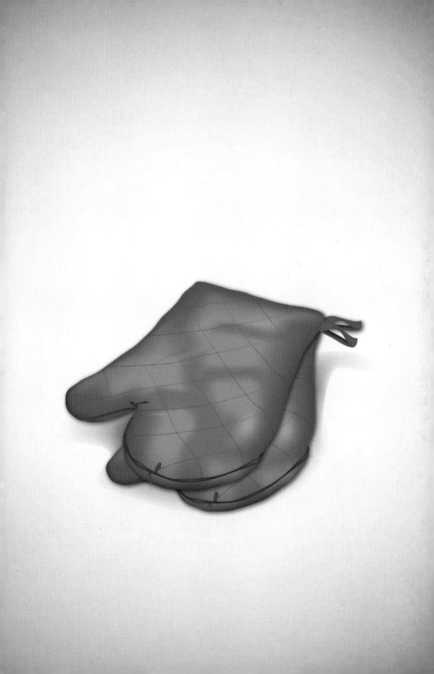

I believe that when you challenge people with an unfamiliar technique, or a new flavor, or an interesting ingredient, it makes them think. And when people think, they learn. From my perspective, any time you cook and you reach a moment when you are uncomfortable, you have to figure it out. Then, you learn something. And it's a good feeling.
—CHRIS COSENTINO, *Beginnings*

• • •

At the restaurant, we have perhaps twenty-five vinegars. At home, though, I have just four, which is all you need in your kitchen.
—RENE REDZEPI, in an interview with the *New Zealand Herald*

• • •

We may dine in two or three languages, as Irving Cobb says, and get thin and willowy [. . .] but a wise and solemn gentleman rises to remark that the world is going to the dogs [. . .] and that something ought to be done to bring back the delectable cooking of our mothers and grandmothers.
—AUNT ELLEN, in Joanna Pruess's *Griswold and Wagner Cast Iron Cookbook*

• • •

Back then, all people did was cook on Sundays because they didn't have refrigerators. You went to the market, bought food fresh, and cooked it that day. You were always in the kitchen.
—MARK VETRI, *Rustic Italian Food*

• • •

As while other passions in your life may, at some point, begin to bank their fires, the shared happiness of good homemade food can last as long as we do.
—JENNI FERRARI-ADLER, *Alone in the Kitchen with an Eggplant*

• • •

There's nothing like a home-cooked meal—nothing! When people ask me what the best restaurant in L.A. is, I say "Uh, my house!" It's more intimate. Food can connect people in a forever sort of way.
—GIADA DE LAURENTIIS

• • •

My mother was a good recreational cook, but what she basically believed about cooking was that if you worked hard and prospered, someone else would do it for you.
—NORA EPHRON

• • •

Cooking for people is an enormously significant expression of generosity and soulfulness, and entertaining is a way to be both generous and creative. You're sharing your life with people. Of course, it's also an expression of your own need for approval and applause. Nothing wrong with that.
—TED ALLEN

• • •

The cool thing is that now that people have made this evolution where cooking is cool, people are doing it on weekends, they're doing their own challenges. It's back to cooking. And it's real cooking.
—EMERIL LAGASSE

• • •

Cookbooks are modern grandmas that teach us old and
new ways of cooking.
—TODD ENGLISH, *The Figs Table*

• • •

I always wondered why the makers leave housekeeping and
cooking out of their tales. Isn't it what all the great wars and
battles are fought for—so that at day's end a family may eat
together in a peaceful house?
—URSULA K. LE GUIN, *Voices*

• • •

The kitchen's a laboratory, and everything that happens there
has to do with science. It's biology, chemistry, physics. Yes,
there's history. Yes, there's artistry. Yes, to all of that. But
what happened there, what actually happens to the food is
all science.
—ALTON BROWN

• • •

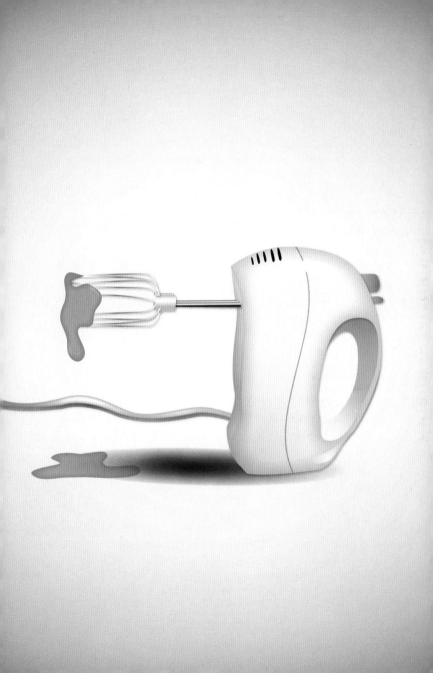

Male egos require constant stroking. Every task is an achievement, every success epic. That is why women cook, but men are chefs: we make cheese on toast, they produce *pain de fromage*.
—BELLE DE JOUR, *The Further Adventures of a London Call Girl*

• • •

The chances of liking what you make are high, but if it winds up being disgusting, you can always throw it away and order a pizza; no one else will know.
—JENNI FERRARI-ADLER, on making dinner for one, *Alone in the Kitchen with an Eggplant*

• • •

The chef who cooks without a song on his lips cannot hope to infuse the right carefree improvisatory note into his art.
—JAMES HAMILTON-PATERSON, *Cooking with Fernet Branca*

• • •

Life is not a recipe. Recipes are just descriptions of one person's take on one moment in time. They're not rules. People think they are. They look as if they are. They say, "Do this, not this. Add this, not that." But, really, recipes are just suggestions that got written down.
—MARIO BATALI

• • •

I love to feed other people. [. . .] Cooking gives me the means to make other people feel better, which in a very simple equation makes me feel better. I believe that food can be a profound means of communication. [. . .] My Gruyere cheese puffs straight from the oven say, "I'm glad you're here. Sit down, relax. I'll look after everything."
—ANN PATCHETT, from the essay "Dinner for One, Please, James"

• • •

A good meal is like a present, and it can feel goofy, at best, to give yourself a present. On the other hand, there is something life affirming in taking the trouble to feed yourself well, or even decently. Cooking for yourself allows you to be strange or decadent or both.
—JENNI FERRARI-ADLER, *Alone in the Kitchen with an Eggplant*

• • •

Do not allow watching food to replace making food.
—ALTON BROWN

• • •

The funny thing about Thanksgiving, or any big meal,
is that you spend twelve hours shopping for it then go
home and cook, chop, braise, and blanch. Then it's gone in
twenty minutes and everybody lies around sort of in a sugar
coma and then it takes four hours to clean it up.
—TED ALLEN, *The Food You Want to Eat*

• • •

[My mother] taught me that a woman in the kitchen isn't a
symbol of domesticity, but of empowerment.
—GAIL SIMMONS, *Talking with My Mouth Full*

• • •

The only time to eat diet food is while you're waiting for the
steak to cook.
—JULIA CHILD

• • •

6

FRIENDS AND FAMILY

Most meals are better when they're eaten in good company.
The food may be perfectly seasoned, the wine may be
wonderfully paired, and the waiter may be on his game—but
if there's no one there to share the experience (or the dessert!),
was the meal really *that* good? Mealtimes should be spent
with the ones we love—the ones who will listen when we talk
about our days, offer advice when we seek it, and hopefully
help clear the tables and dry the dishes before dessert is
served. The quotes in this section reflect upon the joy that
comes with passing the salt and pepper, whether you're
helping make dinner or eating it.

————

I'm gaining weight, and I do blame my kids. [. . .] Have you
seen what a six-year-old wants to eat? "I'll have a slice of
pizza, chocolate milk, and a lollipop." Like they are on some
drug-induced munchies binge. "For dinner, get me mac and
cheese, a handful of pretzels, and half of a cupcake."
—JIM GAFFIGAN, *Dad Is Fat*

• • •

Good cooking brings back memories of something lost, something from the past. On a rainy day, a boring afternoon, you think of your mother and the French toast that she made for you as a child. You make it right at that moment and she's there with you again.
—JEAN-MARIE RIGOLLET, *Creating Chefs*

• • •

Our own grandmothers were classic examples of a bygone era. Marvelous cooks, they prepared delicious cakes and breads by adding a pinch of this and a dash of that. [. . .] Jane once watched her grandmother prepare batter [. . .] "How much flour do you add?" asked Jane. "Until it looks just right," was her grandmother's reply.
—BARBARA GIBBS OSTMANN and JANE L. BAKER, *The Recipe Writer's Handbook*

• • •

I think back to my childhood all the time, and as most people would say, the memories always take me to the kitchen table— telling secrets to my mother, sipping cauliflower soup with my dad and sister, or scarfing down the Pasta with my lifelong best friends.

—ALYSSA SHELASKY, *Apron Anxiety*

• • •

My pop got into a motorcycle accident and was in the hospital for weeks. My grandpa came over and started cookin' all this Italian food. It was the best thing that ever happened to me!

—Overheard by FRANCIS LAM at the San Genaro Street Fair in New York's Little Italy, "Fried-Cheese Epiphany at a Street Fair," as featured on Salon.com

• • •

Good food ends with good talk.
—GEOFFREY NEIGHBOR

• • •

Sharing food with another human being is an intimate act that
should not be indulged in lightly.
—M. F. K. FISHER, American food writer

• • •

May your days be filled with seasonal fresh foods and your
kitchen stocked with the essentials to prepare the foods you
love for the people you cherish.
—KATHY TIERNEY, CEO of Sur La Table, *Things Cook Love*

• • •

You're shopping, you're cooking, you're getting together with family, you're eating food that's bad for you, you're eating more food that's bad for you, and of course you're eating food that's bad for you.
—JIM GAFFIGAN, on holidays, *Dad Is Fat*

• • •

The Sunday dinner—or any leisurely meal with family or friends—brings out so many stories in people that it gives you a deeper connection to everyone at the table. Somehow, it also gives you a deeper connection to the food itself.
—MARK VETRI, *Rustic Italian Food*

• • •

After a good dinner one can forgive anybody, even one's own relations.
—OSCAR WILDE, *A Woman of No Importance*

• • •

Every lesson I learned as a kid was at the dinner table. Being Greek, Sicilian, and Ruthenian—we are an emotional bunch. It is where we laughed, cried, and yelled—but most importantly, where we bonded and connected.
—MICHAEL SYMON

• • •

My mother's menu consisted of two choices: take it or leave it.
—BUDDY HACKETT, American comedian

• • •

I like to think of a recipe as your mother or grandmother at
your elbow, leading you through a new experience.
—ELIZABETH BAIRD, food editor, *Canadian Living*

• • •

If God had intended us to follow recipes, he wouldn't have
given us grandmothers.
—LINDA HENLEY

• • •

A crust eaten in peace is better than a banquet partaken in anxiety.
—AESOP

• • •

Food is our common ground, a universal experience.
—JAMES BEARD

• • •

When I look at a recipe card I see the person who wrote it, and sometimes more. [. . .] Recipe cards and other handwritten documents tell so much more of a story. May I suggest that you sit down and write out a favorite recipe and send it to someone.
—DEBORAH MADISON, "The Case for Handwriting," as featured on ZesterDaily.com

• • •

Food brings people together on many different levels. It's nourishment of the soul and body; it's truly love.
—GIADA DE LAURENTIIS

• • •

When I'm home, the heart and soul of our family is in the kitchen. Growing up, my parents both worked, so dinnertime was for family—the TV was off. I think it's important to grab that time and really make it special, even after a tough day.
—CAT CORA

• • •

I had rather be shut up in a very modest cottage, with my books, my family, and a few old friends, dining on simple bacon, and letting the world roll on as it liked, than to occupy the most splendid post which any human power can give.
—THOMAS JEFFERSON

• • •

My mother instilled in me a love of her kitchen and an appreciation of home, but also the courage to leave it. She made it clear that food opens up the world to you. Food can be comforting, but it can also take you far outside the comfort zone.
—GAIL SIMMONS, *Talking with My Mouth Full*

• • •

7

DINING OUT

Most people eat out for three main reasons: to celebrate, to get out of making dinner at home, or to satisfy a craving for a particular item they can't duplicate in their home kitchens.

Luckily, eateries of all shapes and sizes exist that can meet the expectations of every occasion. French bistros are perfect for romantic anniversary dinners. Fast-food chains with ball pits are great for kids' birthday parties. And ice cream trucks parked conveniently a block away are the perfect way to end long, hot summer days. These quotes reflect on the experience of dining out, whether at a three-star restaurant, a twenty-four-hour diner, or the bar on your corner where impromptu class reunions are held every weekend.

———

People don't go out to eat to be good: they go out to celebrate. They don't necessarily want "healthy" food: they want choices of food that they can't or won't make at home. [. . .] If they can get healthy food that tastes phenomenal, there's no reason to tell them that it also happens to be good for them.
—FRITZ PASQUET, *Creating Chefs*

• • •

Have you noticed that the children's menu [at some restaurants] is exactly the same as the bar menu? Burger, hot dog, pizza. If you put the children's menu at the bar, people wouldn't even notice. "Oh, cool. I can color this menu while I drink this beer and wait for my chicken strips."
—JIM GAFFIGAN, *Dad Is Fat*

• • •

The first thing you notice about a restaurant's menu is how high up the food chain the chef has dared to climb and which foods on the lower rungs he or she has chosen to exclude.
—JEFFREY STEINGARTEN, *The Man Who Ate Everything*

• • •

The hors-d'oeuvre is the first magisterial movement of a culinary symphony that continues to the very end without a false note. Just when you've reached the ultimate with a particular course, another follows to surpass it.
—FERNAND POINT

• • •

We can eat something and trigger a memory. [. . .] But you have to be a diner who wants to be transported, to bring that childlike openness to the table. You have to want to submit to the illusion.
—WYLIE DUFRESNE to FRANCIS LAM, "The Flavorist Conversations," from Salon.com

• • •

A good meal is like a symphony. You start out with that overture and *Boom!* [. . .] It calms down a bit as you have your salad; then you start building again as you go through the entrée. [. . .] All the other components of the dish start playing, the high notes here, the low notes there, and *Bam!* The dessert. The Grand Finale.
—GLENN HUMPHREY, *Creating Chefs*

• • •

La grande cuisine must not wait for the guest; it's the guest who must wait for la grande cuisine.
—FERNAND POINT, *Ma Gastronomie*

• • •

Sushi Etiquette

According to Chef Masaharu Morimoto, "To the sushi novice, nothing seems simpler than sushi—a morsel of fish, often uncooked, on top of a fat finger of rice. The sushi chef forms *nigiri sushi* so quickly, so effortlessly, that you'd be forgiven for assuming there is not much to the craft. But these are deliberate gestures, developed over years of practice. And preparing rice and fish that will make my customers swoon is anything but simple."

This is true of many of us—we really don't know how much time it takes, how much skill is required, how important the relationship is between the restaurateur and the vendors who sell him or her fish, rice, and other ingredients.

The majority of customers in sushi or Japanese restaurants are also unaware of some of the guidelines for eating sushi. Some are listed here for your reference. Next time you visit a Japanese restaurant, keep these in mind—especially if you're seated right at the sushi bar!

1. Lay off the soy sauce. The higher the quality of sushi, the more likely the chefs took their time composing a well-balanced bite. That bite should be tasty enough that it does not require additional soy sauce.

2. Don't mix the wasabi (the green stuff) with your soy sauce. Similar to the guideline listed previously for soy sauce, the chef has prepared you a roll (or other preparation) he or she believes is well-seasoned. Adding additional heat to the food you're given will take away from the natural flavors already presented to you.

3. Eat the pickled ginger (the pink stuff) between bites. This is included with sushi to cleanse your palate between bites—especially if you've ordered multiple types of sushi of varying flavors and ingredients. Don't tear it up or place it on top of your sushi.

4. Open wide. Sushi is not meant to be nibbled—place the piece in your mouth whole and chew. Don't break it apart, don't cut it in half, don't take a bite and put it back on your plate. As previously mentioned, each piece is prepared so that you receive the best bite every time. Don't overcomplicate it.

Rules adapted from the book Morimoto: The New Art of Japanese Cooking

• • •

Insanity hovered close at hand, like an eager waiter at an expensive restaurant.
—ARUNDHATI ROY, *The God of Small Things*

• • •

In my opinion, sexiness comes down to three things: chemistry, sense of humor, and treatment of waitstaff at restaurants.
—RHODA JANZEN, *Mennonite in a Little Black Dress*

• • •

A man who goes into a restaurant and blatantly disrespects
the servers shows a strong discontent with his own being.
Deep down he knows that restaurant service is the closest
thing he will ever experience to being served like a king.
—CRISS JAMI, poet and author of *Luke Wood*

• • •

All great deeds and all great thoughts have a ridiculous
beginning. Great works are often born on a street corner
or in a restaurant's revolving door.
—ALBERT CAMUS, author of *The Stranger*

• • •

One eats with the fingers those which are dry.
—EMILY POST

• • •

Great restaurants are, of course, nothing but mouth-brothels.
There is no point in going to them if one intends to keep one's
belt buckled.
—FREDERIC RAPHAEL, American screenwriter and novelist

• • •

The menu is not the meal.
—ALAN WILSON WATTS, British philosopher

• • •

If he is thin, I will probably dine poorly. If he is both thin and
sad, the only hope is in flight.
—FERNAND POINT, on judging unfamiliar restaurants by
examining their chefs, *Ma Gastronomie*

• • •

8

ON THE LINE

Fernand Point once said, "In all professions without doubt, but certainly in cooking, one is a student all his life." Professional cooks are constantly learning about new ingredients, new techniques, new flavor combinations—it never stops. The culinary world is always changing; old becomes new and new becomes . . . something totally different. The universe cooks live in is a precarious one, from insane hours and sweltering heat to low pay and seared, scarred forearms. Regardless, many in this profession wouldn't give up the sleepness nights and achy knees and feet for any other type of job. This section provides a glimpse into the minds of men and women who spend their lives in professional kitchens.

———

Restrain the chef and you restrain humanity. Set him free and you release creativity. The passions infused into plated foods enter the populace. Food is fuel for the human body; and artistically crafted and presented food is fuel for the soul—a symbiotic sustenance of ideals.
—RONALD JOSEPH KULE, *Chef Tell*

• • •

Recipes are only guidelines. You have to use your
natural-born skills as a human being to taste a dish. It is
the cook who makes the difference.
—RENE REDZEPI, in an interview with the
New Zealand Herald

• • •

The cuisinier loses his reputation when he becomes indifferent
to his work.
—FERNAND POINT, *Ma Gastronomie*

• • •

"There are two days you never forget," Ron Desantis told me. "Your birthday and the day you earn your CMC [Certified Master Chef title]." This from a man married with two children.
—MICHAEL RUHLMAN, *The Soul of a Chef*

• • •

One of the Most Important Introductions in American Restaurant History

I entered the French Laundry kitchen and saw a tall lanky man sweeping the floor. His back was toward me and he didn't hear me enter, so he kept doing his job for a few seconds. I peered past him looking for chef Keller, waited a few seconds for the sweeper to notice me, and when he didn't, approached him. "I'm Grant Achatz, here for a tryout. Is chef Keller in?"

"Yeah. That's me," he said, letting out a laugh. "You're early, Grant."
—From *Life, On the Line*

• • •

We are very much a profession that looks out after their own. Despite the overwhelming number of chefs out there in the world, for some reason chefs feel a respect and kinship toward one another that connects us all.
—JANETTE SINCLAIR, *Creating Chefs*

• • •

Owning a restaurant is a grueling, self-vandalizing profession [. . .]
—ALYSSA SHELASKY, *Apron Anxieties*

• • •

I began to hear from professional-chef friends [. . .] that no self-respecting chef would admit to using cookbooks. But there's a lie tucked inside that attitude: pro chefs, whenever they're dissing recipes, forget to mention that they've all cooked other chefs' recipes thousands of times while coming up through the ranks.
—DANIEL DUANE, "How to Become an Intuitive Cook," as featured in *Food & Wine*

• • •

I feel a recipe is only a theme, which an intelligent cook can play each time with a variation.
—JEHANE BENOÎT, food writer

• • •

Given the stress and the work involved [. . .] I ask Flory,
"Why do these people do it?"
"We always reach for what's beyond our grasp," he says. [. . .]
"It is in our nature. Otherwise we'd be in a *sea of mediocrity*
that's out there."
—A conversation between MICHAEL RUHLMAN and
CHEF ANTON FLORY about working in a kitchen,
in *The Soul of a Chef*

● ● ●

A good cook is the peculiar gift of the gods. He must be a
perfect creature from the brain to the palate, from the palate
to the finger's end.
—WALTER SAVAGE LANDOR, English writer and poet

● ● ●

What struck me about the restaurant was "the push." [. . .]
What I didn't know was that it was actually going to save my
life. That drive, that tenacity, that dedication that I took at that
restaurant [. . .] It helped me get through a pretty
ridiculous battle.
—GRANT ACHATZ, on how working at The French Laundry
helped him fight life-threatening cancer later in life,
Life, On the Line

• • •

Every chef wasn't a madman. Most weren't, in fact. But many
were and are [. . .] a little twisted in the dark spaces of their
brain. They had to be. They worked in a different world with
different rules.
—MICHAEL RUHLMAN, *The Soul of a Chef*

• • •

I've cooked for a variety of well-known people, but cooking for celebrities is no more or less important than any other cooking you do. Your food should come out as your best no matter who is sitting at the table.
—TIM FIELDS, *Creating Chefs*

• • •

The consensus among cooks is that the dividing line between having fun and not having fun in the kitchen is whether you have the most suitable tool for the job.
—MARIE SIMMONS, *Things Cooks Love*

• • •

Do you know why some restaurants have tablecloths?

Nick Kokonas: "I suppose it's because it feels luxurious. Fine white linens look and feel good. They are soft to the touch, beautifully made . . ."

Grant Achatz: "No, not really. It's because the table under the tablecloth is shitty. It's usually a piece of plywood bound to a wobbly base that is cheap and barely balanced. You may not recognize that consciously, but you know it, you can feel it."

—From *Life, On the Line*

• • •

No chef actually practices science, of course; they engage in a craft, because they have to produce: the kitchen is, after all, a laboratory. There, inevitably, chemical and physics experimentation is constantly under way.
—ALBERT SONNENFELD, in the foreword to Hervé This's *Kitchen Mysteries*

• • •

Lunatics and madmen aren't drawn to cooking; chefs become that way because of the conditions of the form, conditions you could measure in hours, in actual degrees Fahrenheit.
—MICHAEL RUHLMAN, *The Soul of a Chef*

• • •

For those who know food, cooking is not a job, it's a love affair.
—CAROL W. MAYBACH, *Creating Chefs*

• • •

You can't truly respect the grind of the restaurant business until you've lived with it. That said, it is rough.
—ALYSSA SHELASKY, on dating a chef, *Apron Anxieties*

• • •

You've got to understand. [. . .] It's a different environment
in here from out there.
—THOMAS KELLER to MICHAEL RUHLMAN, on the
front versus the back of the house, *The Soul of a Chef*

• • •

The Secret of Good Cooking is: First, be a critical judge—
know excellent cooking from poor cooking; Second, find a
fascination in the science, and become thoroughly familiar
with "what and what not to do"; Third, find a genuine pleasure
in the practice—masking the basic recipes and the operation
and control of your Range—and above all, THINK.
—AUNT ELLEN, in Joanna Pruess's *Griswold and Wagner
Cast Iron Cookbook*

• • •

For chefs, who couple artistry with blue-collar labor, every day is a patchwork of small battles.
—AMANDA HESSER, *Eat, Memory*

• • •

Learning to cook food perfectly, applying the proper technique to the food in hand, is the way to revere its simplicity. Its depth and complexity come from learning to taste in isolation, and then to layer flavors to add interest and meaning to the dish.
—CAROL W. MAYBACH, *Creating Chefs*

• • •

I believe that precision in cooking is not about who can construct the most meticulously perfect recipe, but who can master their skill and techniques so well that they can apply them to more or less anything with great results.
—MAGNUS NILSSON, *Fäviken*

• • •

No chef should bad-mouth any other.
—GRANT ACHATZ, *Life, On the Line*

• • •

To be a great cook, you need the best ingredients, the correct tools, and a patient, thoughtful approach to cooking that allows you to get the timing, temperature, and technique right. Cooking is also an art form, and there is plenty of room for personal expression in every recipe.
—*In the Kitchen with Le Cordon Bleu*

• • •

I liked the energy of cooking, the action, the camaraderie. I often compare the kitchen to sports and compare the chef to a coach. There are a lot of similarities to it.
—TODD ENGLISH

• • •

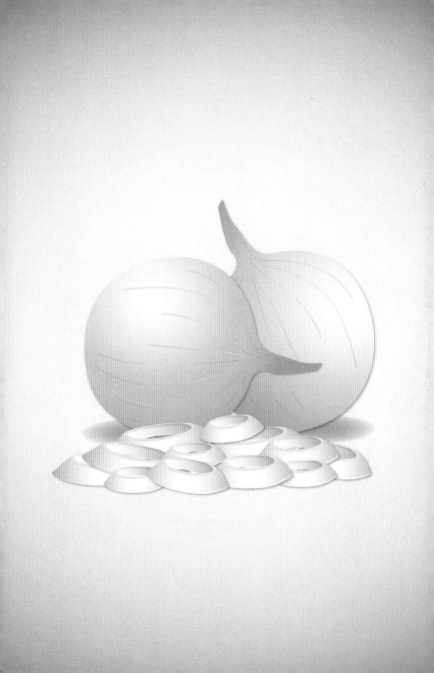

We don't graduate chefs, we graduate culinarians, who then may become chefs.
—GLENN HUMPHREY, *Creating Chefs*

• • •

The Grind: In the kitchen we often refer to "The Push." In our world, the push is the exact opposite force of the grind. You have to push to overcome the tendency to grind to a halt. It is a willful act.
—GRANT ACHATZ, *Life, On the Line*

• • •

You don't come into cooking to get rich.
—GORDON RAMSAY

• • •

I equate [being the chef] to a conductor conducting an orchestra. The conductor is the one who's getting billing. You don't expect the conductor to jump in and start playing the instruments. In fact, if he does, you're in trouble. Same thing with a chef.
—TOM COLICCHIO to SCOTT RAAB, *Esquire*

• • •

"Executive chef" makes this sound like a corporate office.
This is a kitchen—not a corporation.
—THOMAS KELLER to GAIL SIMMONS, from *Talking with My Mouth Full*

• • •

Obviously, [a chef is] a leader; we all know that. But a real chef
can fix any problem that comes up in the course of the day,
and that is the cutoff point, that's when a chef is really a chef.
—LYDIA SHIRE to CHARLOTTE DRUCKMAN, *Skirt Steak*

• • •

9

WORLD CUISINES

Food can be comforting and food can be breathtaking. It can also be informational—a gateway to learning about cultures other than our own. Sure, the American spin on many dishes in US restaurants may make the bowls of ramen, dishes of curry, and scoops of gelato "less authentic," but regardless of their authenticity, they're still delicious and they still offer us a chance to take a few steps outside our comfort zones. Hopefully the quotes in this section inspire you to doublethink the cheeseburger or steak and try the borscht or uni next time you get the chance. (And if you find that type of cuisine isn't your "thing," at least you can say you tried something new!)

―――――

"Well," Claire said, "at least we have tacos. Everything goes better with tacos."
—RACHEL CAINE, *Bitter Blood*

• • •

Patriotism is a longing for the food of our homeland.
—LIN YUTANG, Chinese poet-statesman

• • •

I don't think it's a real cuisine because you don't do much.
—JULIA CHILD, on Italian cooking

• • •

[It's] just you eating in places you've never been. "Why don't
we eat something, then we'll go get something to eat? Then
we should see that thing we're supposed to see; they probably
have a snack bar [. . .] But after that, we definitely gotta go out
and get something to eat."
—JIM GAFFIGAN, on vacations, *Dad Is Fat*

• • •

What interests me is how the quality of cooking in this country can be followed from a period of simplicity and function to one of goodness and bounty, then to age of elaboration and excess, back again to functional (and . . . mediocre) eating. Finally, we hope, we are now in another epoch of gastronomic excellence.
—JAMES BEARD, on American diets, *James Beard American Cookery*

• • •

I still feel that French cooking is the most important in the world, one of the few that has rules. If you follow the rules, you can do pretty well.
—JULIA CHILD

• • •

Nothing is more tiresome than listening to regional zealots claim that a particular area's specialty can't taste "authentic" outside its birthplace. [. . .] The point is, great food is about ingredients and execution, not location.
—ANDREW KNOWLTON, "The Food List," *Bon Appétit*

• • •

Soul food, it would seem, depends on an ineffable quality. It is a combination of nostalgia for and pride in food of those who came before.
—JESSICA B. HARRIS, *High on the Hog*

• • •

Cuisines taken by emigrants to new lands have always changed to adapt to the ingredients available to them, giving us such odd and delicious dishes.
—FRANCIS LAM at the San Gennaro Street Fair in New York's Little Italy, "Fried-Cheese Epiphany at a Street Fair," as featured on Salon.com

• • •

The tradition of Italian cooking is that of the matriarch. This is the cooking of grandma. She didn't waste time thinking too much about the celery. She got the best celery she could and then she dealt with it.
—MARIO BATALI

• • •

The borough [of Brooklyn] has become an incubator for a culinary-minded generation whose idea of fun is learning how to make something delicious and finding a way to sell it.
—*THE NEW YORK TIMES*

• • •

Leave it to the Italians to come up with an ingenious way to cook chicken perfectly. But under a brick? The chicken ends up flat as a pancake. The meat is as moist as can be and the skin is incredibly crisp.
—JOANNE WEIR, *Weir Cooking*

• • •

The couscous concept is simple and it is brilliant . . . When served together—the grain and the stew—the result is extraordinary. With the possible exception of bisteeya, couscous is the crowning achievement of Moroccan cuisine.
—PAULA WOLFERT, *Couscous and Other Good Food from Morocco*

• • •

You must play to a culture's strengths and not order a
cataplana of paella when in Green Bay, Wisconsin.
—HEIDI JULAVITS, "Turning Japanese," *The New York Times*

• • •

Did I mention that New York is the greatest restaurant town
on Earth? We may not have an indigenous cuisine, unless
you count dirty-water hot dogs, but we sure have the cultural
critical mass for an amazing variety of ethnic cuisine.
—PETER KAMINSKY, *Culinary Intelligence*

• • •

England has three sauces and three hundred different
religions, while France has three religions and three hundred
different sauces.
—FRENCH PROVERB

• • •

The passion of the Italian or the Italian-American population
is endless for food and lore and everything about it.
—MARIO BATALI

• • •

Every country, every region, has its local specialties about
which it's rash to say, "they're not very good," because nature
supplies every taste.
—FERNAND POINT, *Ma Gastronomie*

• • •

It's really important to be a good guest, because the table is the
best reflection of a nation and the fastest way into that culture.
[. . .] You can't be squeamish or hesitant. [. . .] Now is not the
time to say "I'm a vegetarian" or "I'm lactose intolerant."
—ANTHONY BOURDAIN to DIANNE JACOB,
on fearlessly eating internationally, *Will Write for Food*

• • •

"Gotham" has long been at the forefront of America's culinary vanguard. [. . .] New York City is a melting pot, a wonderland of so-called ethnic eats. It's famously home to the finest of fine dining, too. And it's a city in love with food from the nearby countryside.
—TRACY RYDER and CAROLE TOPALIAN, *Edible*

● ● ●

Spanish chefs prefer cooking with earthenware, the most ancient kind of cooking utensil known to man, but they have a hard time explaining why. "The food just tastes better," they are likely to say.
—PENELOPE CASAS, *Delicioso*

● ● ●

To eat well in England you should have breakfast three times a day.
—W. SOMERSET MAUGHAM, British author

● ● ●

10

FOOD AND WINE

Some people love drinking just as much as they love eating. They love the fizz of champagne, the taste of wine, and the scent of hops. They find comfort in a glass of red or a frosty mug of lager at the end of a long day. They recognize that pairing just the right type of beer, wine, or sake with a meal can make flavors on the dish stand out among the others. (The right pairing can *absolutely* take an already good meal to the next level.) Today, people write recipes for cocktails as often as they do for desserts. Chefs are developing restaurants based on what they plan to offer at the bar and are making their alcoholic beverages the main features on their menus. In this section, we offer thoughts on the consumption of alcohol (and essential nonalcoholic beverages like coffee) in a respectable way.

———

One of the most important things that distinguish man from other animals is that man can get pleasure from drinking without being thirsty.
—FERNAND POINT, *Ma Gastronomie*

• • •

A meal without wine and without friends is like a heart
without love.
—WILLIAM SONSTEIN, former wine advice columnist
for the *Inquirer*

• • •

One of the most insidious myths in American wine culture is
that a wine is good if you like it. Liking a wine has nothing to
do with whether it is good. Liking a wine has to do with liking
that wine, period.
—KAREN MACNEIL, *The Wine Bible*

• • •

Misquoted!

Though largely attributed to Ben Franklin, the quote "God made beer because he loves us and wants us to be happy," has never appeared in an authoritative source with Franklin's name attached.

Historians and wine aficionados believe that this beer quote was spun time and time again from the following excerpt, which appeared in a letter Franklin wrote to friend André Morellet in 1779:

"Behold the rain which descends from heaven upon our vineyards; there it enters the roots of the vines, to be changed into wine; a constant proof that God loves us, and loves to see us happy."

• • •

To know is to be able to name.
—ÉMILE PEYNAUD, *Le Goût du Vin (The Taste of Wine)*

• • •

Great wine is about nuance, surprise, subtlety, expression,
qualities that keep you coming back for another taste.
Rejecting a wine because it is not big enough is like rejecting
a book because it is not long enough, or a piece of music
because it is not loud enough.
—KERMIT LYNCH, *Adventures on the Wine Route*

• • •

What's in a name?

Wine enthusiasts from the United States and Great Britain
refer to the droplets of wine that tumble quickly down the
inside of the glass after the wine has been swirled as *legs*.

The Spanish call them *tears*.

The Germans call them *church widows*.

Despite the difference in names and cultures, most people
fall victim to the same misunderstanding: they believe
these drops are indicative of a great wine. However, the
number or look of these droplets has nothing to do with
how "great" the wine is. Instead, they tell a totally different
story—one of scientific phenomena, rates of evaporation,
surface tension, and water versus alcohol content.

Without Mona, Hanna felt like a great outfit without matching
accessories, a screw-driver that was all orange juice and no
vodka, and an iPod without headphones. She just felt wrong.
—SARA SHEPARD, *Pretty Little Liars*

• • •

The sign was spray-painted in Arabic and English, probably
from some attempt by the farmer to sell his wares in the
market. The English read: Dates–best price. Cold Bebsi.
"Bebsi?" I asked.
"Pepsi," Walt said. "I read about it on the Internet. There's no
'p' in Arabic. Everyone here calls the soda Bebsi."
"So you have to have Bebsi with your bizza?"
"Brobably."
—RICK RIORDAN, *The Throne of Fire*

• • •

In so complex a world, buying a bottle of wine for dinner should be one of life's easier (and happier) tasks.
—KAREN MACNEIL, *The Wine Bible*

• • •

Tea tempers the spirits and harmonizes the mind, dispels lassitude and relieves fatigue, awakens thought and prevents drowsiness, lightens or refreshes the body, and clears the perceptive faculties.
—CONFUCIUS

• • •

Ah, the cocktail! Epitomized by the languorous promise of a shimmering Martini, surrounded by glamour and ritual, cocktails are back in style, riding a wave of nostalgia. . . . Over the course of the twentieth century, the cocktail evolved into an art form.
—MITTIE HELLMICH, *Ultimate Bar Book*

• • •

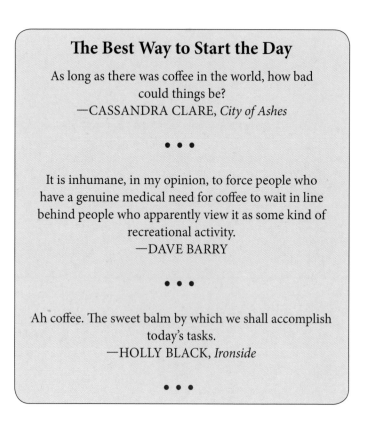

The Best Way to Start the Day

As long as there was coffee in the world, how bad
could things be?
—CASSANDRA CLARE, *City of Ashes*

• • •

It is inhumane, in my opinion, to force people who
have a genuine medical need for coffee to wait in line
behind people who apparently view it as some kind of
recreational activity.
—DAVE BARRY

• • •

Ah coffee. The sweet balm by which we shall accomplish
today's tasks.
—HOLLY BLACK, *Ironside*

• • •

The only vampires I've ever seen are the Goths trying to get
a glimpse of Anne Rice's house, who drink strawberry sodas
and tell each other it's blood.
—SHERRILYN KENYON, *Infinity*

• • •

The key to mixing the perfect drink lies in the attention
to detail—the drinks being poured should be balanced
proportionately and perfectly executed. Making a drink can
be an artistic exercise, an orchestration of ingredients and
technique, and a mixologist is viewed
as a knowledgeable maestro.
—MITTIE HELLMICH, *Ultimate Bar Book*

• • •

Did you know . . .?

A glass a day may keep the doctor away.

According to Jeffrey Steingarten's *The Man Who Ate Everything*, drinking a moderate amount of alcohol frequently—perhaps even up to one glass of red wine *per day*—may actually help your health, rather than hinder it.

"People who drink moderate amounts of alcohol on a regular basis have far fewer heart attacks than those who do not drink at all. And since moderate drinking carries very few risks (except on the highway), moderate drinkers generally live longer than people who do not drink."

So next time you're curled up with a book or at a table with friends, raise your glass to living longer, happier, more fulfilling lives and drink up!

• • •

Did you know . . .?

The winemaking process for reds and whites is both similar and different. For example, while both red and white wines require the picking of grapes and the removal of stems (for both wines, this step is optional), red wines are created via a process of crushing grapes—juice, skin, seeds and all. The process of making white wines is better described as pressing instead of crushing, and the skins of the grapes are removed before placing them in the tank.

Once the fermentation process begins for red wine, the winemaker must pay close attention to the grape skins, being sure to push them down or pump them over the fermenting liquid. Once the fermentation process is complete, red wine is placed in a barrel and left to age. Occasionally, the barrels may be racked.

White wine, however, is oftentimes left to sit after fermentation to establish contact with the lees. Once this occurs, the winemaker has the option of cold stabilizing the wine and placing it in barrels to age before bottling. These final two steps are not necessary for white wine.

The older wine gets, the more it changes color. In fact, red wines get lighter with age, while white wines become darker as time passes.

• • •

The chef Paul Bocuse defines thusly the ideal wine: it satisfies perfectly all five senses; vision, by its color; smell, by its bouquet; touch, by its freshness; taste, by its flavor; and hearing, by its *glou-glou*.
(*Glou-glou* is the sound of the wine disappearing down our throats.)
—An anecdote GORDON M. SHEPHERD overheard in France, from *Neurograstronomy*

• • •

Drink seems positively naked without some visual accompaniment. . . . The garnish is where you can really get creative, and it's the perfect visual cue to help set the tone of your cocktail.
—MITTIE HELLMICH, *Ultimate Bar Book*

• • •

Light, medium, and full-bodied wines feel in the mouth like skim milk, whole milk, and half-and-half, respectively.
—KAREN MACNEIL, *The Wine Bible*

• • •

The Nine Most Popular, Classic Types of Wine

Red	White
Pinot Noir	Chenin Blanc
Syrah	Riseling
Merlot	Chardonnay
Cabernet Sauvignon	Sauvignon Blanc
	Sémillion

• • •

Presentation plays an important role in the much-ritualized cocktail experience, visually enticing our palates with the promise of refreshment. There is no denying that the right glass will add a touch of elegance to even the simplest drink.
—MITTIE HELLMICH, *Ultimate Bar Book*

• • •

How to Order Your Drink

Getting the attention of the bartender is often difficult enough. When he or she approaches you, if you're unfamiliar with bar lingo, you may lose your chance to order if you can't spit out what you want immediately. Familiarize yourself with these terms to be sure the bartender hears you correctly and you pay for the drinks you and your guest actually wanted.

Dry

A term meaning "not sweet." This term is normally used to refer to wine or Martinis.

Neat

No ice, water, or any other ingredients; served "straight up," unchilled and on its own.

On the Rocks

Served over ice. This term is normally used when ordering liquor or mixed drinks.

Perfect

Equal parts dry and sweet vermouth. This term is normally used when ordering specific cocktails, such as the Perfect Martini.

Straight

Served without any liquor or mixers; oftentimes served in a chilled glass or over ice. This normally applies to a spirit. Occasionally, the bartender may add a splash of club soda or water.

Up

Served in a cocktail glass without ice; typically shaken in a cocktail shaker and strained into a glass.

• • •

The mouthfuls most discussed taste best.
—GRIMOD DE LA REYNIÈRE, eighteenth-century socialite

• • •

"What do you want?"
"Just coffee. Black—like my soul."
—CASSANDRA CLARE, *City of Bones*

• • •

Candy is dandy, but liquor is quicker.
—OGDEN NASH, *Hard Lines*

• • •

I won't eat any cereal that doesn't turn the milk purple.
—BILL WATTERSON, *The Authoritative Calvin and Hobbes*

• • •

Be a child again. Flirt. Giggle. Dip your cookies in your milk.
Take a nap. Say you're sorry if you hurt someone. Chase
a butterfly. Be a child again.
—MAX LUCADO, *When God Whispers Your Name*

• • •

Some things just aren't meant to go together. Things like oil
and water. Orange juice and toothpaste.
—JIM BUTCHER, *Death Masks*

• • •

How to Talk Wine

According to Hervé This, "Because wine is a liquid, we can treat it differently from solid food when we taste it." Wine first appeals to our eyes—we often study its robe, or the decreasing thickness of liquid that slides down the inside of the glass after we tilt it, in addition to its highlights and tears/legs/church widows. Then, we pay attention with our noses by breathing in the wine's scent, or bouqet. Finally, we use our mouths to taste the wine many times over, analyzing its many notes.

When it comes time to discuss what we've seen, smelled, or tasted, it's important to be as specific as possible. Try the words in the following lists and confidently speak to other enthusiasts at your next wine tasting or pairing—or use it to impress your next date!

The robe may appear . . .

Beautiful amber, brilliant, intense, light, limpid, raspberry, yellow straw.

The highlights may be . . .

Cherry, garnet, green, old rose, purple, rosé, ruby, yellow.

The tears may be . . .

Clear, viscous, yellow.

The bouquet may smell like . . .

Caramel, flowers, game, green pepper, green wood, leather, mushrooms, raspberry, red or black currant, ripe or fresh fruits, roasted almonds, smoke, tobacco, violet, undergrowth or earth; complex, developed, fruity, pleasant, present, racy, rustic, slightly acidic, wild.

The wine may taste . . .

Aggressive, ample, balanced, charming, drinkable, fatty, firm, fleshy, fortified, frank, fruity, full, harsh, heady, heavy, light, lively, pungent, rich, round, silky, smooth, soft, solidly built, structured, supple, voluminous, young, winey.

If you don't like your wine, it may be because it tastes . . .

Flat, musty, oxidized, séché, or short.

• • •

[Attending sommelier school] opened up to me a completely new world, a strange world in which it seemed that the more you learned, the less you understood.
—MAGNUS NILSSON, *Fäviken*

• • •

Drink wine. This is life eternal. This is all that youth will give you. It is the season for wine, roses and drunken friends. Be happy for this moment. This moment is your life.
—OMAR KHAYYÁM

• • •

11

SWEET TOOTH

Cannoli, key lime pie, and chocolate pudding . . . Parfaits, cinnamon and sugar doughnuts, and peanut butter cups . . . A mountain of ice cream drizzled with hot fudge, sprinkled with peanuts, covered in whipped cream, and topped with a cherry (or two!). If your mouth's not watering, something's clearly wrong with you—or so our fellow dessert lovers would say! This section is for those who love to lick the batter from spoons, sip sugary drinks through candy straws, and can't say no to a second piece of pie after epic holiday dinners.

———

Candy is the currency of children. Kids collect it, trade it, and hoard it. It's how parents bribe their kids. It's how annoying kids get friends.
—JIM GAFFIGAN, *Dad Is Fat*

• • •

When shit brings you down, just say "f— it," and eat yourself some motherf—ing candy.
—DAVID SEDARIS, *Me Talk Pretty One Day*

• • •

Dear Ben & Jerry's: Just so you know, a pint of Chunky Monkey *is* considered one serving. Please either adjust your nutritional labels or create a smaller package.
—JEN LANCASTER, *Such a Pretty Fat*

• • •

A party without cake is just a meeting.
—JULIA CHILD

• • •

Life is uncertain. Eat dessert first.
—ERNESTINE ULMER, American writer

• • •

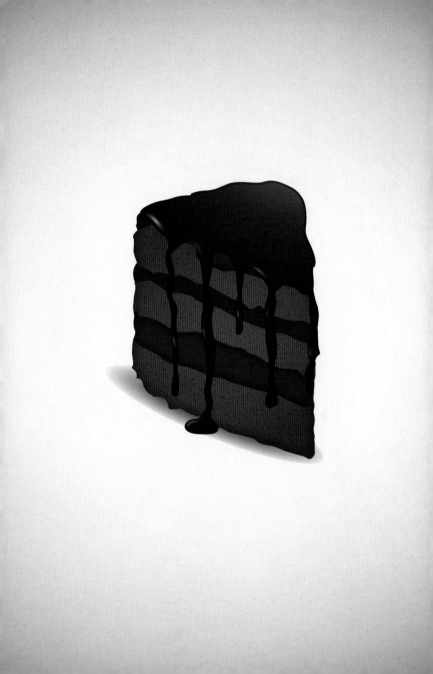

It takes forty muscles to frown, and only twelve to jam a
cupcake in your mouth and get over it.
—SARAH OCKLER, *Bittersweet*

• • •

Who doesn't love Popsicles? They're cool, they're fun, and they
remind you of your childhood.
—NATHALIE JORDI, co-owner of People's Pops, to
SHERRI EISENBERG, *Food Lovers' Guide to Brooklyn*

• • •

To become a good cook, you must first try your hand at
pastries, because that is the best school for learning
correct proportions.
—AUGUSTUS ESCOFFIER

• • •

A man who attaches great importance to dessert after a good
meal is a fool who spoils his spirit with his stomach.
—JEAN DE LA VARENNE, Cook to Louis XIII

• • •

All human beings are born with a sweet tooth—and with good reason. Sugar equals energy.
—PETER KAMINSKY, *Culinary Intelligence*

• • •

Chocolate is the world's favorite flavor. There is a mystery, excitement, and wickedness associated with chocolate you'll find in no other food.
—TISH BOYLE and TIMOTHY MORIARTY,
Chocolate Passion

• • •

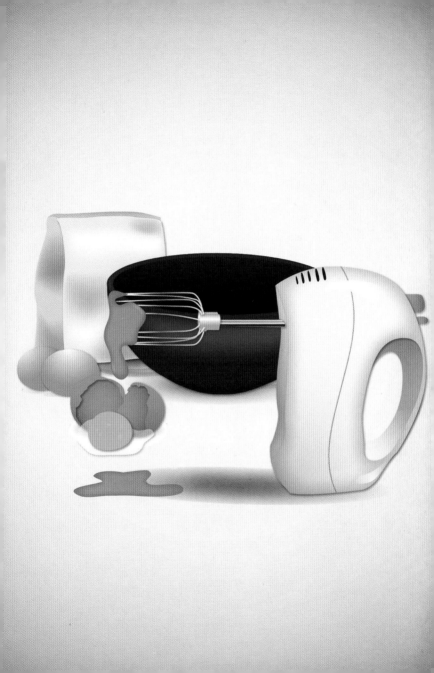

Seize the moment. Remember all those women on the *Titanic*
who waved off the dessert cart.
—ERMA BOMBECK, American humorist

• • •

Strength is the ability to break a chocolate bar into four pieces
with your bare hands—and then eat just one of those pieces.
—JUDITH VIORST, *Love & Guilt & the
Meaning of Life, Etc.*

• • •

It tastes like spring!
—ANNA GORDON'S assistant upon tasting carrot cakes
at Gordon's The Good Batch, as told to SHERRI EISENBERG,
Food Lovers' Guide to Brooklyn

• • •

I might not have a boyfriend, but I have cupcakes, and those tasty bastards haven't let me down yet.
—L. H. COSWAY, *Painted Faces*

• • •

You're only human. You live once and life is wonderful so eat the damn red velvet cupcake!
—EMMA STONE

• • •

Any cupcake consumed before 9 a.m. is, technically, a muffin.
—BRIAN P. CLEARY, author of *Hairy, Scary, Ordinary*

• • •

Sometimes in the midst of all your boy drama, you just need a cupcake.
—SUSANE COLASANTI, *So Much Closer*

• • •

It is always sad when someone leaves home, unless they are simply going around the corner and will return in a few minutes with ice-cream sandwiches.
—LEMONY SNICKET, *Horseradish: Bitter Truths You Can't Avoid*

• • •

Ice-cream is exquisite. What a pity it isn't illegal.
—VOLTAIRE

• • •

Like magic, she felt him getting nearer, felt it like a pull in the pit of her stomach. It felt like hunger but deeper, heavier. Like the best kind of expectation. Ice cream expectation. Chocolate expectation.
—SARAH ADDISON ALLEN, *The Sugar Queen*

• • •

I want to lose weight by eating nothing but moon pies, which have significantly less gravity than earthier foods such as fruits and vegetables.
—JAROD KINTZ, *I Want*

• • •

What people eat last, they remember first.
—FRIEDEMAN PAUL ERHARDT, on dessert,
as quoted in Ronald Joseph Kule's *Chef Tell*

• • •

We must have a pie. Stress cannot exist in the presence
of a pie.
—DAVID MAMET, *Boston Marriage*

• • •

Every time I look into his eyes I just want to take the ice
cream or whatever I've got in my hand and rub it into his face.
That's how much I like him.
—BANANA YOSHIMOTO, *Goodbye Tsugumi*

• • •

Whoever, by the way, thought a tiny candy bar should have been called Fun Size was a moron. Trust me there's nothing more fun than hearing a full size Snickers from one house drop into your bag onto the full size Three Musketeers you got at the last house.
—GLENN BECK, on Halloween candy, *Glenn Beck Radio Program*

• • •

Wait. Why am I thinking about Krispy Kremes? We're supposed to be exercising.
—MEG CABOT, *Big Boned*

• • •

Do you want me to call you Celery Stick instead of Cupcake or Honey-Pie? It just doesn't inspire the same warm and fuzzy feelings.
—RICHELLE MEAD, *The Indigo Spell*

• • •

12

FOOD PHILOSOPHY

We don't have to tell you that food means different things to different people. Some see cooking as an art form, others see it as a means to spark political debates, some use it as a muse, and still others simply view it as a way to quiet the rumblings in their stomachs. This section features ideas about how food affects every aspect of life from some of the greatest minds in history (food-related and otherwise), as well as many of the popular minds of today. These speakers believe that much can be learned from food, whether we're growing it, making it, or eating it.

———

What I say is that, if a man really likes potatoes, he must be a pretty decent sort of fellow.
—A. A. MILNE, author of *Winnie-the-Pooh*

• • •

The best time for planning a book is while you're doing the dishes.
—AGATHA CHRISTIE, English crime writer

• • •

There are some things, after all, that Sally Owens knows for certain: Always throw spilled salt over your left shoulder. Keep rosemary by your garden gate. Add pepper to your mashed potatoes. Plant roses and lavender, for luck. Fall in love whenever you can.
—ALICE HOFFMAN, *Practical Magic*

• • •

The pleasure of eating, when done in moderation, is the only act that is not followed by tiredness.
—JEAN ANTHELME BRILLAT-SAVARIN

• • •

As far as cuisine is concerned, one must read everything, see everything, hear everything, try everything, observe everything, in order to retain in the end just a little bit.
—FERNAND POINT, *Ma Gastronomie*

• • •

If truth were told, in the culinary arts, as in the art of living, excellent, sustained achievement is accomplished only by superb execution of training basics and strict attention to detail in the face of harsh realities, plus imagination.
—RONALD JOSEPH KULE, *Chef Tell*

• • •

Food is the metaphorical spoonful of sugar that helps the proverbial medicine go down.
—CHARLOTTE DRUCKMAN, *Skirt Steak*

• • •

If fear of food continues, it will be the death of gastronomy in the United States.
—JULIA CHILD, in an interview with *The New York Times*

• • •

The pleasure of sitting down to a good meal is not limited to just eating what's set in front of you. It can also be about the sensations or memories associated with it.
—DAVID LEBOVITZ, in the foreword to *Will Write for Food*

• • •

Tell me what you eat and I will tell you what you are.
—JEAN ANTHELME BRILLAT-SAVARIN, *The Physiology of Taste*

• • •

Eating is so personal. It's about your family, it's about your culture, it's about your daily routine—it's very personal. But it is also this amazing branch which provides kids the chance to start thinking about access and privilege, region and globalization, and all of these types of things.
—ERIN SHARKEY to CHRISTA GLENNIE SEYCHEW, for *Edible*

• • •

Ask not what you can do for your country. Ask what's
for lunch.
—ORSON WELLES

• • •

This can be an art, and there are times when it is in the hands
of certain individuals. [. . .] But it's an incredibly capricious
art in that it doesn't last. Ten minutes after it's served, it's gone.
[But] I was wrong—because cuisine lives on in memory.
—NORMAN VAN AKEN to ANDREW DORNENBURG
and KAREN PAGE, authors of *Culinary Artistry*

• • •

It's absolutely unfair for women to say that guys only want one
thing: sex. We also want food.
—JAROD KINTZ, *$3.33*

• • •

Chefs can be extremely creative, but our form of art doesn't last—except in cookbooks. In painting, imagination is key. But in food, you must use your senses to create, in a way, a "virtual reality."
—DANIEL BOULOUD to ANDREW DORNENBURG and KAREN PAGE, authors of *Culinary Artistry*

• • •

Eat and drink to live not to die.
—ELIJAH MUHAMMAD, *How to Eat to Live*

• • •

When I look back on it, I wonder quite why [my parents] were so insistent that pigs' trotters weren't for me, and I think the answer is because they'd decided pigs' trotters weren't for them. Trotters were peasant food and my parents were no longer prepared to be peasants.
—GEOFF NICHOLSON, *Tin House*

• • •

We are indeed much more than what we eat, but what we eat can nevertheless help us to be much more than what we are.
—ADELLE DAVIS, American author and nutritionist

• • •

Great food is like great sex. The more you have the more you want.
—GAEL GREENE, American restaurant critic

• • •

One cannot think well, love well, sleep well, if one has not dined well.
—VIRGINIA WOOLF

• • •

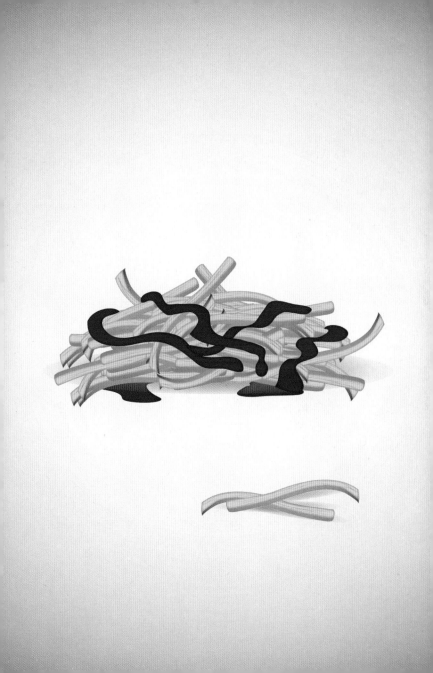

Life is a bowl of cherries. Some cherries are rotten while others are good; it's your job to throw out the rotten ones and forget about them while you enjoy eating the ones that are good!
—C. JOYBELL C.

• • •

Governing a great nation is like cooking a small fish—too much handling will spoil it.
—LAO TZU

• • •

I have long believed that good food, good eating is all about risk. Whether we're talking about unpasteurized Stilton, raw oysters, or working for organized crime "associates," food, for me, has always been an adventure.
—ANTHONY BOURDAIN, *Kitchen Confidential*

• • •

Nobody's an optimist before breakfast.
—P. G. WODEHOUSE

• • •

Chefs and cooks, whether amateur in the home kitchen
or professional behind the stoves, anyone, in short, with
more than the slightest curiosity, should want to know how
things work.
—ALBERT SONNENFELD, in the foreword to Hervé This's
Kitchen Mysteries

• • •

Finding opportunities to cook in new places, seeking out food
artisans who preserve their heirloom methods of making
products, visiting organic farmers' markets, eating family-style
or at least lingering over dinners that last for hours in homes
or restaurants with local people—all these experiences
afford us not only great pleasure, but also the opportunity to
embrace diversity.
—CAROL W. MAYBACH, *Creating Chefs*

• • •

If I were to die and be reincarnated as a vegetable, I would like to be a fava bean, hiding inside that little stem, living inside a velvet room.
—TODD ENGLISH, *The Figs Table*

• • •

Today many of us crave the comfort of the familiar in one form or another. That yearning is most obvious in our food choices: simplicity is the new sophistication and fussy fare seems dated.
—JOANNA PRUESS, *Griswold and Wagner*
Cast Iron Cookbook

• • •

As a culture, we seem to have arrived at a place where whatever native wisdom we may once possessed about eating has been replaced by confusion and anxiety [. . .] How did we ever get to a point where we need investigative journalists to tell us where our food comes from and nutritionists to determine the dinner menu?
—MICHAEL POLLAN, *The Omnivore's Dilemma*

• • •

Fishing is the only philosophical activity that fills you up.
—NORWEGIAN PROVERB

• • •

Embarrassment felt a lot like eating chili peppers. It burned in the back of your throat and there was nothing you could do to make it go away. You just had to take it, suffer from it, until it eased off.
—SARAH ADDISON ALLEN, *The Sugar Queen*

• • •

Life is like an ice cream cone; you have to lick it one day at a time.
—CHARLES M. SCHULZ

• • •

There is nothing particularly wrong with salmon, of course, but like caramel candy, strawberry yogurt, or liquid carpet cleaner, if you eat too much of it you are not going to enjoy your meal.
—LEMONY SNICKET, *The Ersatz Elevator*

• • •

You can tell a lot about a fellow's character by his way of eating jellybeans.
—RONALD REAGAN

• • •

Life is a combination of magic and pasta.
—FEDERICO FELLINI

• • •

If more of us valued food and cheer and song above hoarded gold, it would be a merrier world.
—J. R. R. TOLKIEN

• • •

Without such a thing as fast food, there would be no need for slow food, and the stories we tell at such meals lose most of their interest. Food would be . . . well, what it always was, neither slow nor fast, just food.
—MICHAEL POLLAN, *The Omnivore's Dilemma*

• • •

A gourmet is just a glutton with brains.
—PHILIP W. HABERMAN

• • •

"Real" foods—even if somewhat embellished—don't require mental gymnastics to appreciate.
—JOANNA PRUESS, *Griswold and Wagner Cast Iron Cookbook*

• • •

The proof of the pudding is the eating.
—MIGUEL DE CERVANTES SAAVEDRA, author of *Don Quixote*

• • •

Hard work IS its own reward. Integrity IS priceless. Art DOES feed the soul.
—MARCUS SAMUELSSON, *Yes, Chef: A Memoir*

• • •

There are two activities in life in which we can lovingly and carefully put something inside of someone we love. Cooking is the one we can do three times a day for the rest of our lives, without pills. In both activities, practice makes perfect.
—MARIO BATALI

• • •

Lives are snowflakes—unique in detail, forming patterns we have seen before, but as like one another as peas in a pod. (And have you ever looked at peas in a pod? I mean, really looked at them? There's not a chance you'd mistake one for another, after a minute's close inspection.)
—NEIL GAIMAN, *American Gods*

• • •

Never be afraid to try something different.
—HENRY FONDA to CHEF FRIEDEMAN PAUL
ERHARDT, as quoted in Ronald Joseph Kule's *Chef Tell*

• • •

I don't like gourmet cooking, or "this" cooking, or "that"
cooking. I like good cooking.
—JAMES BEARD

• • •

Even a blind hen makes a delicious soup.
—SWEDISH PROVERB

• • •

We light the oven so that everyone may bake bread in it.
—JOSÉ MARTÍ, *Nuestra América y Otros Escritos*

• • •

Shame is a soul eating emotion.
—C. G. JUNG

• • •

When engaged in eating, the brain should be the servant of
the stomach.
—AGATHA CHRISTIE

• • •

Those Quoted

Resources

Every effort has been made to identify the original source of the quotes that appear on these pages.

Aside from the books cited throughout the text, we also relied on articles in magazines such as *Bon Appétit* and interviews that appeared in newspapers such as the *New York Times*.

In some cases, we also referred to the websites such as GoodReads .com, BrainyQuote.com, and SearchQuotes.com to confirm the wording, primary source, or speaker of various quotations.